PHIP'S FARM

CHARLES RIVER

1st British Shuttle

2nd British Shuttle

Fox Hill

COMMON

LEGEND

1   PROVINCE HOUSE
2   GREEN DRAGON TAVERN
3   JOSEPH WARREN'S HOUSE
4   PAUL REVERE'S HOUSE
5   THE "COCKEREL"
6   CHRIST CHURCH
7   ROBERT NEWMAN'S HOUSE
8   THE BURYING PLACE
9   WINDMILL
10 CLARKE'S' WHARF

Frog Lane

Pleasant St.
Hollis St.
Clough St.
Orange St.

Castle St.

ROXBURY FLATS
[DRY AT LOW WATER]

NECK

Orange St.

L.E.F.

Dawes

LECHMERE PT.

BUNKER'S HILL

Breed's Hill

CHARLES RIVER

CHARLESTOWN

Revere

HMS Somerset

N

Spring St.
Gravel St.
Leveret's St.
Wiltshire
Green Lane
Hawkins St.
Hilliers St.
Sudbury St.
Cambridge St.
Staniford St.
Temple St.
George St.

MILL POND

Ferry Way
9   8
Charles St.
Salem St.
Cross St.
Back St.
Middle
North St.
Lynn St.
Prince St.
Bennet's Alley
North Battery St.
Ship St.
6
5
4
North Sq.   Sun Ct.
Fish St.
10

Beacon
Hill
Beacon St.

Hanover St.
Cold Lane
Back St.

2
3

School St.
Treamont St.
Queen St.
Brattle St.
Dock Sq.
Union St.
Ann
Fish St.

Long Acre
Jackson's St.
Cornhill
King St.
Water St.

Marlborough St.
Summer St.
Bishops Alley
Milk St.
Water St.
Kilby St.
Long Wharf

d'Acosta's
Pasture

Field
South St.

Cow Lane
Belchers Lane
Battery March
Battery March
Fort
Hill

THE HARBOR

BOSTON   APRIL 18
1775
IN NEW ENGLAND

TWO
if by
SEA

In this dramatic story, Leonard Everett Fisher brings to life two of the most crucial hours in American history—from nine to eleven on the evening of April 18, 1775.

Would war break out between the thirteen American colonies and the British government? Four men in Boston held the key: Doctor Joseph Warren, Mr. Paul Revere, General Thomas Gage, and Sexton Robert Newman. In suspenseful detail Mr. Fisher follows each of the four men through the two fateful hours.

Words and pictures are based on a careful study of the historical records, as well as Mr. Fisher's first-hand acquaintance with Boston's Revolutionary streets and buildings. Skillfully he combines text and illustrations to show how the actions of four men affected the future of all Americans.

TWO
if by
SEA

written and illustrated by
Leonard Everett Fisher

RANDOM HOUSE · NEW YORK

For helpful suggestions in the preparation of this book, the author and the publisher are grateful to Richard B. Morris, Professor of History, Columbia University.

973.3
Fi

CONTENTS

Those who expect to reap the blessings of freedom must undergo the fatigue of supporting it.
    —*Thomas Paine* (1777)

Prologue

At noon June 1, 1774, a dull peel of muffled church bells began to roll across the thirteen American colonies in a melody of sympathy for the people of Boston. Great Britain had closed the port of Boston as punishment for the "Tea Party"—the incident in which some patriots, disguised as Indians, dumped 342 chests of English tea into Boston Harbor. They were protesting the new Tea Act and its unwanted tax.

The London government decreed that no food or goods could be shipped in or out of the city by sea until the people of Boston paid for the spoiled tea—something they were not about to do. A British naval squadron and 4,000 troops were already there to enforce the blockade. Great Britain, so many times provoked by colonial defiance, was now ready to destroy Boston's commerce in order to crush her rebellious spirit.

With the shutdown of the port, all Boston business came to a halt. All work stopped. Half the people of Boston—some 7,000—went jobless. Soon they would not even be allowed to fish in their own waters.

In London, Parliament acted further to strengthen British authority in Massachusetts. Henceforth, persons accused of serious crimes in Massachusetts could be tried in London rather than in Boston. Moreover, Massachusetts colonists would be ruled by a council appointed by the King instead of by their own freely elected lawmakers. Finally, Bostonians would have to provide quarters for British troops in their own homes if regular army barracks were unavailable.

All the other American colonies viewed these laws—these "Intolerable Acts"—as a blow to their own liberties. Boston's danger was their danger. The crippling of Boston by England was more than most American colonists could bear.

Food poured into the stricken city by the only land route—the Neck. Americans everywhere began to arm and drill. They met in public to protest and in secret to plan a rebellion. Independence seemed to be the only solution to the years of bickering between England and her colonies. Voices of moderation were quieted.

By the spring of 1775 the smell of battle was in the air. But the stubborn colonists waited for the British to make the first move.

They did—on the evening of April 18, 1775.

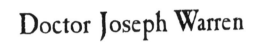

Doctor Joseph Warren

Doctor Joseph Warren's house on fashionable Hanover Street loomed silent and shapeless in the night as William Dawes and a companion hurried toward it. The two men, holding on to their wind-whipped tricorns, ran, walked, and stumbled with breathless urgency.

The clocks of Boston had just struck nine as they crossed Union Street. The full moon was yet to rise. A cold, gusty wind was at their backs, pushing and shoving them down the bleak and empty street. A driving rain that had softened much of New England earlier in the morning had long since drifted away. Now this wild breeze came out of the starry blackness and swept inland across the bay. It flattened the swaying sea grasses of the harbor islands, raced over Copp's Hill, filled the narrow lanes of Boston's North End, and buffeted the city beyond.

The two men broke into a dead run a few yards from the house and reached the front door within seconds. They were members of an active revolutionary group, the Sons of Liberty. Doctor Joseph Warren, Boston's revolutionary leader, had sent for Billy Dawes and a companion. Now they were here, unseen by any of the roving patrols of British soldiers who had orders to keep the townspeople indoors on this night.

Gasping, the two men leaned against the door, almost fading into the face of the dark building.

"Listen," whispered the sagging, winded Dawes.

The faint rattling clank of weapons, mingled with the shuffling of boots, seemed to rise from the cobbled street. The sounds were distant but unmistakable. They seemed to be all around the two men, carried by the careless wind. They were the sounds of British troops assembling at North Square, not a half-mile from where Dawes and his partner now stood. Only minutes before, the two men had been lurking in the shadows near North Square, watching the military activity.

In the candle-lit front parlor of the house, Doctor Warren was seated at an old, battered walnut desk, staring at a blank page in his daily medical journal. He had some entries to make, but the words would not come. He could not even recall the remedies he had prescribed for the several patients he had seen during the day. His mind was on the British troops. He knew that they were about to leave Boston and march through the blossoming countryside on a mission filled with danger for the American patriots.

Except for a servant, Joseph Warren was alone in the house. His wife, Elizabeth, had been dead for two years. Their four small children were on the Warren farm in Roxbury, a few miles south of Boston. In fact, the modestly furnished house did not belong to the doctor. He had rented it some years before to be close to the Green Dragon Tavern, the favorite meeting place of the Sons of Liberty.

From this Hanover Street house the tall, brown-haired, broad-shouldered physician sallied forth to heal the sick—and to run the Massachusetts Committee of Safety, the patriots' underground army. As president of the committee, Joseph Warren was one of the three most important radical leaders in Boston. The other two were Sam Adams and John Hancock.

For ten years or more, soft-spoken, penniless Sam Adams was America's most vigorous champion of self-rule. He saw no way to achieve it other than by armed rebellion. Sam Adams was an extremist who brilliantly wrote and preached a doctrine of violent disobedience against British colonial rule. He organized a Committee of Correspondence to relay revolutionary messages, letters, and articles from town to town. He did everything he could to encourage ordinary Americans toward revolution.

Unlike the impoverished politician, Sam Adams, John Hancock was a wealthy merchant. For years he had resented the severe British restrictions on colonial commerce. He defied these laws by smuggling. Once the British captured his ship *Liberty*. Riots followed the incident. Hancock was proclaimed a hero by the mobs.

He was elected to the Massachusetts General Court, the colony's lawmaking body. There he joined with Sam Adams to stir up more trouble for the British. These two radical leaders, Hancock and Adams —both founders of the Massachusetts Sons of Liberty—continued to work together to fan the flames of political unrest.

The Sons of Liberty dealt harshly with anyone who was loyal to the King of England. They enforced the boycott of British goods. Some Massachusetts citizens who bought, sold, or even used British goods were tarred and feathered. Others had their homes and shops torn apart, their possessions hacked to pieces and burned.

The Sons of Liberty held secret meetings. They wore special insignia and used passwords. Each member swore on the Bible that he would not reveal or discuss the business of the organization with anyone except Sam Adams, John Hancock, Doctor Joseph Warren, and Doctor Benjamin Church.

Benjamin Church, like Joseph Warren, was a popular Boston physician. He publicly sided with the patriots on every important issue. When the British dissolved the General Court, the angered colonists formed a new legislature—the Provincial Congress—and elected Church as one of their representatives. He was a hard-working member of Sam Adams's Committee of Correspondence, and he contributed stinging, patriotic poems to Boston newspapers. Doctor Church, an engaging man, seemed to have as many friends at British headquarters as he had among the patriots—especially among Joseph Warren's Committee of Safety.

The Committee of Safety helped to enforce some of the resistance schemes of the Sons of Liberty. Its chief task, however, was to stockpile arms and ammunition in various Massachusetts towns. These were for use in opposing any military force the British might send against the rebellious colonists. The Committee of Safety also helped to organize the town militias into better fighting units. At the same time, the com-

11

mittee saw to it that every farmer or village craftsman who did not belong to the militia was ready to fight at a minute's notice. These were called "Minutemen."

Nearly every Massachusetts town had a branch of the Committee of Safety. And they all looked to Doctor Joseph Warren to find out whether —and when—British troops were to move out of Boston. The doctor was determined not to disappoint them.

A few months earlier he had organized about thirty North End craftsmen, under the leadership of his friend Paul Revere, into America's first intelligence service. Sometimes called "Warren's Watchers," Revere and his men kept an eye on the British and reported whatever they found out to Warren. There was very little about His Majesty's Boston garrison that the doctor did not quickly learn.

And now, on this Tuesday evening—April 18, 1775—Joseph Warren had received from his watchers the definite word which the people of Boston and the rest of Massachusetts had been expecting for the past few days. Hundreds of British troops were assembling in combat order. "The Regulars were out," and Joseph Warren was anxious to warn the patriots in the countryside.

William Dawes took a deep breath and then pounded the solid oak door with his huge fist.

"Enough man, enough!" his companion cried hoarsely, his face all but hidden behind the thick turns of a muffler. "Do you want the bloody King's Own here, to do our knocking for us?"

"The King's Own, indeed!" replied Dawes. "They're too busy with their muster to pay any mind to us." Again he drove his fist against the door, but the whistling wind covered the heavy sound.

Doctor Warren hurried to the door as the thudding noise continued. He opened it an inch, recognized Dawes, and flung the door open.

"Come in, Billy, quickly now!" said the doctor. "We have work to do this night." He bolted the door and peered at the stranger in the dim light. "Do I know your faceless friend, Billy?"

"No, sir. I do not think so. He's new in the Sons of Liberty, sir. But the truest friend he is, doctor. He's an honest one with a clever eye for

those ruddy lobsterbacks. He can . . ."

"Good, excellent," Warren cut in as he led his visitors into the parlor, motioning to them to sit.

The doctor had so many things on his mind that it did not occur to him to inquire after the man's name. Billy Dawes's word was enough. Time was short. He could not afford to waste any of it. He needed both men—urgently.

"Billy," he asked, "can you get across the Neck and out of Boston, tonight?"

Dawes could not be sure. The Neck—the narrow strip of land connecting Boston to the mainland—was the only land route in and out of the city. Sometimes the tides washed over it, making the Boston peninsula into an island. Moreover, the Neck was fortified. The British Fifty-ninth Nova Scotia Regiment had been there since the previous October, when General Thomas Gage, the governor, had ordered it to the town gate. He wanted to seal off the city against any possible attack by the thousands of defiant colonials who were arming in all the nearby towns and villages.

"Those lobsters in the streets are not out for an evening stroll," Dawes

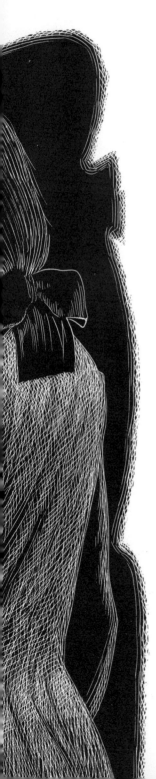

began. "The word is that Gage will have the torch put to Concord by morning. Is this true—"

"That is exactly what he is up to, Billy," interrupted Warren. "At least, I am reasonably sure that he is. He is after our weapons there. He is going to try to disarm us. But we shall fool him, Billy. We shall fool him. He will not find a single musket. I sent Mr. Revere to Concord only this past Sunday to warn our friends there of the coming peril. They should have found another hiding place for our supplies by now."

"Let us pray they have, doctor," Dawes said quietly.

"There is another pressing matter," Warren continued. "I have reason to believe that General Gage has issued arrest warrants for John Hancock and Sam Adams. The charge is treason. Bah! Against whom? The Devil? In any case, these gentlemen are now with Parson Clarke in Lexington. Mr. Revere saw them also on Sunday, alerted them to possible danger, and promised them further word. He prevailed upon them not to return to this unsafe city, fearful as we all are for their lives. They finished their business at the Provincial Congress. There was no reason for them to return here.

"But now we must warn them of the warrants, at once, before they are seized, carried off to London for trial, and then hanged by the neck."

"But you, sir," asked Dawes, "what about you? Gage will not rest till he has done likewise to you, too!"

"Perhaps, Billy," replied the doctor. "But never mind about me. The important thing is for you to get to Adams and Hancock before the British find them. If we can reach the Charlestown side of the river with either a rider or a signal, we shall have another express riding to Lexington from Charlestown. But in all likelihood we shall not be able to get a message across. So you must try for the land route to Lexington— over the Neck and through Roxbury, Brookline, Cambridge, and Menotomy. On your way you must spread the alarm that the Regulars are out. If those troops spill one drop of Yankee blood, we want to have enough of our militia and Minutemen on hand to spill a bit of theirs!"

"Have you any idea when the British will march?" asked Dawes.

"Probably within the hour," replied Warren. "No one knows just how they will depart—across the river by boat or over the Neck by foot. Gage

15

cannot keep his intentions a secret much longer. But I want you to be riding hard for Lexington before they move out. Can you leave now?"

William Dawes stood up, slowly. He stroked his bristly jaw, vacantly looked at the low ceiling, and thought.

If anyone could get through the British guard at the Neck, it was Billy Dawes. For weeks he had been going out there. He did odd jobs for the British—mostly shoe repair and carpentry—sold them terrible liquor more cheaply than they could buy it anywhere else, and generally made himself useful. At times he pretended to be drunk and joined the soldiers' lively horseplay.

The men of the Fifty-ninth liked him. They looked upon him as something of a town character—a harmless rowdy. In fact, he had once beaten a British soldier for annoying young Mrs. Dawes—and the English command had done nothing about it. Apparently the British had no suspicion that Billy Dawes was spying on them.

"Yes," said Billy. "I'll go immediately."

Joseph Warren then turned to the stranger behind the muffler.

"I take it that you know Mr. Revere—Paul Revere, the silversmith— by sight. Do you know his house on North Square?"

"Yes, I do, sir."

"I should like you to fetch him for me. In all likelihood he is at home, waiting for a message from me. If not, find him—the sooner the better. Have him come alone. It will be safer that way."

The stranger arose. "I know, doctor," he said. "North Square was packed with lobsterbacks when you sent for us. It may still be. We were over near Sun Court when your man found us—trying to get a closer look at some of those marines. Anyway, you shall have Mr. Revere, sir, without delay."

Warren was already halfway to the door, telling Dawes where to pick up his horse. He spoke a few words of encouragement to both men and sent them on their way.

Joseph Warren returned to the parlor to wait for Paul Revere. Again he sat down at the writing table and stared at the blank page. Still the words would not come. His head was spinning. Tiny glistening flecks of sweat lined his upper forehead.

Hancock and Adams had to flee Lexington. Dawes or Revere would warn them in time—or would they? Perhaps the British would let Billy through on purpose and then follow him straight to the Clarke house. No! Billy was too clever to let that happen.

What about Joseph Warren himself? Why hadn't the British arrested him by now? They must know that he was still in Boston. With Adams and Hancock in hiding, surely they knew that he, Joseph Warren, was now the chief troublemaker. Were Gage's troops perhaps on their way to Hanover Street at that moment to arrest him?

Warren shook his head as if to shake loose these nagging, gnawing questions. These were the risks. He had to take them even if it meant his arrest, the loss of his life, the orphaning of his children. None of these things was too high a price to pay for liberty.

"So be it," he muttered to himself.

Again the front door shuddered under the dull thuds of someone's fist. Warren stiffened in his chair and waited. There was no further noise. Could it be the British? Would they not be louder, more demanding, more insistent, smashing the door in with rifle butts?

Warren vaulted from his chair and raced for the door. Once more he opened it slightly, gingerly, but a gust of wind tore it from his loose grip.

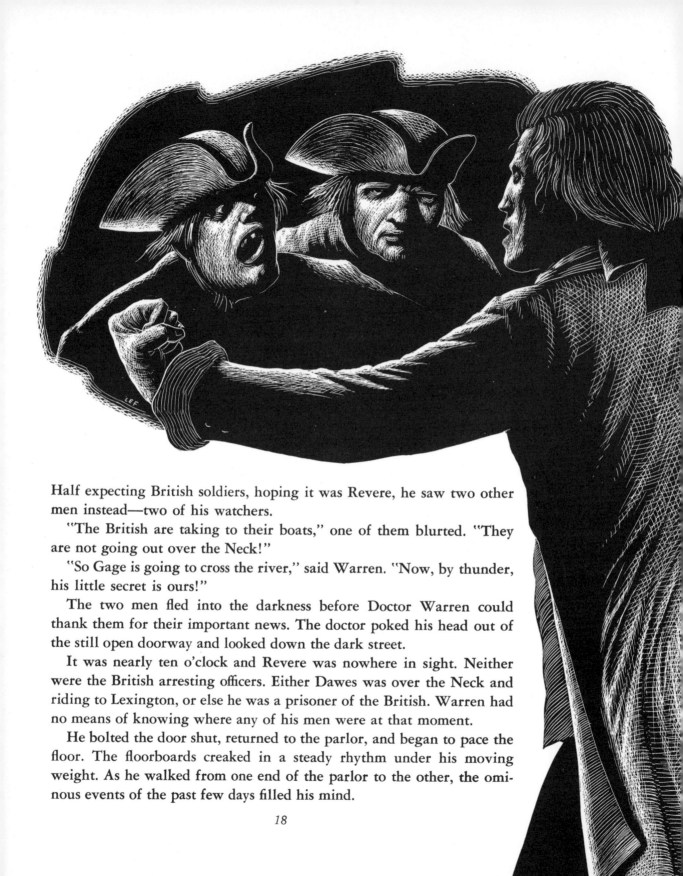

Half expecting British soldiers, hoping it was Revere, he saw two other men instead—two of his watchers.

"The British are taking to their boats," one of them blurted. "They are not going out over the Neck!"

"So Gage is going to cross the river," said Warren. "Now, by thunder, his little secret is ours!"

The two men fled into the darkness before Doctor Warren could thank them for their important news. The doctor poked his head out of the still open doorway and looked down the dark street.

It was nearly ten o'clock and Revere was nowhere in sight. Neither were the British arresting officers. Either Dawes was over the Neck and riding to Lexington, or else he was a prisoner of the British. Warren had no means of knowing where any of his men were at that moment.

He bolted the door shut, returned to the parlor, and began to pace the floor. The floorboards creaked in a steady rhythm under his moving weight. As he walked from one end of the parlor to the other, the ominous events of the past few days filled his mind.

18

Three days earlier—on Saturday, April 15—Joseph Warren learned that General Thomas Gage had ordered about 700 of his best fighting troops to be ready for action. These troops were detached from eleven of the twelve regiments making up the 4,000-man British garrison of Boston. One company of experienced marines, about thirty men, were also placed on special alert. These picked troops represented a sizable fighting force. Warren became concerned about the British intentions.

On Saturday evening, Doctor Warren met with Paul Revere to plan what actions they should take in case General Gage was preparing something more than a practice march. Warren and Revere could not be sure what Gage had in mind. They could only guess.

Sometime after midnight, as the two patriots continued to discuss the situation, Warren's watchers saw about twenty longboats being lowered into the Charles River from H.M.S. *Boyne,* a 64-gun man-of-war, and her sister ship *Asia.* Other watchers reported that the even larger warship *Somerset* had taken up a position midway between Charlestown and the north end of Boston, guarding the 500-yard-wide entrance to the Charles River. At the same time a small frigate, H.M.S. *Lively,* which had brought General Gage to Boston almost a year before, slipped her berth and took up a position in the river. Now Doctor Warren knew that the British were about to begin an assault against the colonists.

Both Joseph Warren and Paul Revere thought that Gage probably wished to destroy colonial military supplies. He had tried that before— not always with success. The two patriots also thought the general intended to arrest the radical leaders—especially Sam Adams, John Hancock, and perhaps themselves.

Neither Warren nor Revere knew exactly when Gage's assault force would move out of Boston. Nor could they be sure which of several military stores the British would seek to destroy—the ones at Charlestown, Watertown, Salem, Worcester, Marblehead, or Concord. But the likeliest target seemed to be Concord. It was the town that stored the largest supply of rebel weapons within easy reach. Moreover, Concord was close to Lexington where Sam Adams and John Hancock were hiding—as the British had reason to suspect.

As the night wore on, Warren and Revere settled on a course of action. At daybreak—Sunday morning—Revere would leave for Lexington and Concord to warn Adams and Hancock and the other patriots there about General Gage's threatening moves. On his way back to Boston, Revere would stop in Charlestown to talk to the leaders of the Committee of Safety there. He would make arrangements to send a message from Boston to Charlestown—across the river—as soon as the British troops began to move.

Early Sunday morning, as planned, Revere rode off to Lexington. Warren could do nothing but wait for his return and hope for further news from his watchers. There was little activity inside Warren's red-brick house on Hanover Street that Sunday. Not much happened on the following day either—April 17. It drizzled on and off.

Everyone was waiting. The British waited to march. The Sons of Liberty waited in their taverns gulping great drafts of ale. Paul Revere, having returned from his trip late Sunday night, waited at home playing games with his youngest children. Joseph Warren waited in his parlor, pacing the floor from time to time.

Now it was Tuesday evening, April 18. The waiting game was over. No one knew how it would all end—least of all Doctor Joseph Warren, president of the Committee of Safety.

Born in Massachusetts of a family that had been in America more than a hundred years, Joseph Warren knew of not a single living relative left in England. Except for one friend in London, neither Warren nor his family had any ties with the Old World.

Educated at Harvard College, Warren belonged to the upper class of colonial life. Yet he cared little for its money, silks, satins, musicales, and polite conversation. He was devoted to medicine and to politics. He had the largest medical practice in Boston. He was a friend to everyone, rich and poor, weak and powerful alike. He was respected and admired by nearly as many loyalists as patriots. His patients included the former royal governor of Massachusetts, Thomas Hutchinson; the patriot lawyer John Adams and his wife Abigail; Billy Dawes, the roughneck North End artisan; the miserable wretches in the poorhouse and the prison.

Like many other patriots, Warren believed that Great Britain was selfish. She took too many of the fruits of the colonists' labor and allowed them too little in return.

Great Britain taxed the colonists without their consent. She refused to listen to their grievances. She refused them the right to elect their own representatives to the Parliament in London. She dissolved their own lawmaking bodies. She limited their manufacture and trade. She quartered troops in their midst over their protests. And, most insulting of all, she treated them like worthless, ill-mannered provincials.

Ever since the Boston Tea Party, which he had secretly helped to organize, Joseph Warren had put himself in the forefront of the drive toward American independence. He confounded the British, stirred his fellow patriots, and moved America closer to being a sovereign nation. In the eyes of the British government, he was a marked man.

Warren had nothing to gain personally by his political activities. Many

patriots were fearful that he had gone too far against the British when he drafted the "Suffolk Resolves"—an angry list of complaints and threats that Paul Revere delivered to the Continental Congress in Philadelphia in September 1774. The Congress adopted the "Resolves."

Warren himself began to think that he should use his energies against the British in the field. He was willing to give up both medicine and politics if the Congress would only make him a general and give him an army to fight the British.

To Joseph Warren the issue was clear. America had to be free and independent. For him there was no choice. America could no longer suffer the abuses handed out by a government 3,000 miles distant. England, he believed, was a foreign power and had no rightful claim upon the people and territory of the thirteen colonies.

Now he paced the parlor floor waiting for Paul Revere—more anxious than ever to start the silversmith patriot on his way with the news that the Regulars were on the move. It was about ten o'clock. Joseph Warren knew that the moment had come for the people of Massachusetts and their allies in the other American colonies to resist English power on American soil—their own soil.

"In God's name," he cried out, "where is Revere?"

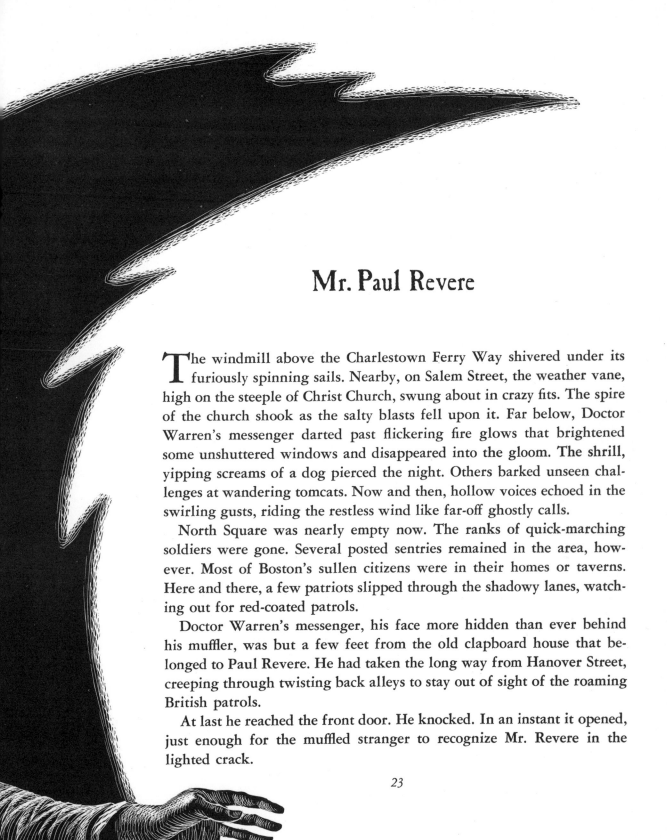

Mr. Paul Revere

The windmill above the Charlestown Ferry Way shivered under its furiously spinning sails. Nearby, on Salem Street, the weather vane, high on the steeple of Christ Church, swung about in crazy fits. The spire of the church shook as the salty blasts fell upon it. Far below, Doctor Warren's messenger darted past flickering fire glows that brightened some unshuttered windows and disappeared into the gloom. The shrill, yipping screams of a dog pierced the night. Others barked unseen challenges at wandering tomcats. Now and then, hollow voices echoed in the swirling gusts, riding the restless wind like far-off ghostly calls.

North Square was nearly empty now. The ranks of quick-marching soldiers were gone. Several posted sentries remained in the area, however. Most of Boston's sullen citizens were in their homes or taverns. Here and there, a few patriots slipped through the shadowy lanes, watching out for red-coated patrols.

Doctor Warren's messenger, his face more hidden than ever behind his muffler, was but a few feet from the old clapboard house that belonged to Paul Revere. He had taken the long way from Hanover Street, creeping through twisting back alleys to stay out of sight of the roaming British patrols.

At last he reached the front door. He knocked. In an instant it opened, just enough for the muffled stranger to recognize Mr. Revere in the lighted crack.

23

"I have come from Doctor Warren, sir," he whispered. "He has urgent business with you—now! Go alone, sir. Hurry!"

"Is there no further word? No signal?" asked Revere, his voice rising with surprise.

"No, no further word, sir. Please, sir, hurry!"

Revere was confused. He expected a different message from Warren. Had something gone wrong? Had word been sent to Charlestown already? Anything was possible. Events were moving rapidly. He must lose no time getting to Warren's to find out what was happening.

"What moves between here and the good doctor?" asked Revere.

"Not much now," came the whispered reply. "The soldiers were like a swelling tide minutes ago. By the sounds of them, they're jamming into the Common. And they're coming from every point in town—from here, the warehouse barracks, Fort Hill, the Neck, Back Street. I wouldn't heed the quiet, sir. There's more Regulars where they came from. No telling how many will be out tonight. You should go now. The moon will soon rise full. Some lobsterbacks are crawling about this very square. A patrol is at the far end and coming this way."

"I know, I know," rasped the stocky figure behind the door. "I can see them for myself."

Warren's messenger did not tell the impatient Revere anything he did not already know or could not guess. He had been in his shop near Clarke's Wharf, about a block away, until shortly before nine o'clock. On the way home he saw some of the troops leave North Square and disappear down Fish Street. They were practically moving past his doorstep. But he was able to slip by the sentries and enter his house without attracting special attention.

There he waited for word from Joseph Warren to tell him what signal to send to Charlestown. Usually even-tempered, Paul Revere stormed about the house, looking out one window, then another, glaring and swearing at the mass of troops in the square.

Now word had come—not to send a signal, but to have another meeting with Joseph Warren.

Although Warren's summons at this late hour was unexpected, Revere had no doubts about going. Always he had done everything the doc-

tor asked of him—and more. He had mounted his horse at least a dozen times to deliver revolutionary messages for the Committee of Correspondence and the Committee of Safety. He had been to Philadelphia, New York, New Hampshire, and numerous other places on rebel business.

Cleverly, he rode express without unnecessarily showing his face to the British high command. The British knew his name. They knew about his radical activities and associations. They knew that he was an important revolutionary. But few if any of the British knew what he looked like.

Fortunately, too, while most of Boston's people had British troops quartered in their homes, the Reveres had none. The family was so large that there was no room to billet a soldier. Paul Revere could come and go without attracting notice.

Revere was a dependable, honest, and tireless worker. Warren knew that he could count on him in any situation. The two men had become fast friends. Not only did they trust each other on revolutionary matters, but also on personal affairs. Doctor Warren attended to the various illnesses that afflicted the Revere family. Revere used his skillful hands

to make and fit two false teeth for Warren. Plainly, Joseph Warren considered Paul Revere one of the most useful and reliable men in Boston.

The previous Sunday morning, in accordance with the plan he and Dr. Warren had formed, Paul Revere had slipped out of Boston. He rode to Lexington at an easy pace, so as not to arouse any suspicion. At Lexington he warned Adams and Hancock to prepare for trouble. From there he rode on to Concord, where he advised the patriots to hide the military supplies in a safer place—and quickly.

Revere returned to Boston by way of Charlestown, where he met with Colonel William Conant of the Committee of Safety. Revere told Conant and several others that the British were preparing to mount some kind of military action against the colonists. The minute the British began to move, a messenger from Boston—probably Revere himself—would try to cross the river to Charlestown with the news.

Revere and the Charlestown patriots knew that a messenger might not be able to reach Charlestown from Boston. The British might even stop the ferryboat. There was already a nine o'clock evening curfew on all boat crossings to the mainland. Also, with the *Somerset* stationed in

the river between Charlestown and Boston's North End, the messenger might not be able to get across undetected.

As an additional precaution, to make sure that the Charlestown patriots would learn that the "Regulars were out," they were to keep watch for a signal in the steeple of Christ Church on Copp's Hill. The church with its high spire was the most familiar landmark in Boston to people on the Charlestown shore. If the British began to march out over the Neck, one lantern would be shown. If they began to cross the river to the mainland, two lanterns would be shown.

Early Sunday evening, Paul Revere returned to Boston by ferry.

Later that evening, though tired from his long day's ride, Revere held a secret meeting at the Green Dragon Tavern for a few Sons of Liberty. He and the others agreed that Robert Newman, the young sexton of Christ Church, would light the signal lanterns when the time came. John Pulling and Tom Barnard would help him. Josh Bentley and Tom Richardson would try to get Revere across the river to Charlestown in Revere's rowboat, which he kept hidden along the shore for just such an emergency.

Finally, Revere explained the plan that he and Doctor Joseph Warren had formed. Warren would send word to Revere telling him when and how the British were moving out. Revere would set off immediately for the Charlestown shore. On his way he was to let Rob Newman know how many lanterns to light.

A few more details were then discussed and the meeting came to an end.

That had been the plan on Sunday. Now it was Tuesday evening. The British had begun to move. Revere stood in the doorway of his house, wondering why the doctor had summoned him to Hanover Street instead of ordering him to Charlestown, as planned.

"You'd better be off," Revere directed his caller, who was tugging his muffler closer to the bridge of his nose as he nervously eyed the approaching patrol.

"No! Wait!" Revere added quickly. "Go around to the back of Rob Newman's house. You know it—across from Christ Church. Be careful.

A number of the King's officers are settled in there. You'll find an open window. Stay quiet until you see either Rob or his mother approach the window. They'll be on the lookout for me. Tell either one that I have been delayed. But have Rob meet me at the corner of Sheafe and Salem. Go now! Quickly!"

The messenger left without further word. He took one more look over his shoulder at the advancing patrol, turned the first corner, and melted into the night.

Revere slowly, soundlessly, closed the door and headed for the back of his house as the unseeing patrol swept by. Close at his heels were his dog and his eldest son, 15-year-old Paul. Young Paul, standing near the door, had heard everything that passed between his father and the messenger.

Revere's mother, creaking back and forth in a rocking chair, had watched the quick scene at the doorway but had heard none of the whispered conversation. Rachel, Revere's second wife, was upstairs with her baby son. So were Paul Revere's five daughters by his first wife, who had died two years earlier.

Revere slapped a brown hat on his head as he opened the rear door. In the next second he was outside in the bracing wind without an overcoat —too hurried to worry about the cold night air.

Young Paul watched the muscular silhouette of his father fade into the dark as he made his way through their backyard to the rear of the Cockerel—the New North Brick Congregational church. The boy stood in the open doorway, holding the family dog. Visions of high adventure crowded his mind. At last, he stepped back and closed the door, shutting it all off—the dark night, the wind, the rising moon, the figure of his coatless father.

The Cockerel—so called because of its brass rooster weather vane— was the church of the brawling North End craftsmen, often called "mechanicks." It faced Middle Street, a thoroughfare joining Hanover at the Mill Creek drawbridge. The creek was a short canal that cut north and south across the upper section of the Boston peninsula. It separated the North End from the rest of Boston.

Here in the North End, fiery Will Molyneaux's "Liberty Boys" and Captain Mackintosh's "South End Gang" used to engage each other in many street brawls. Somehow Sam Adams had been able to unite the rival street gangs into his own club for political disorders—the boisterous Sons of Liberty.

The Cockerel, too, was the church of Paul Revere's baptism forty years earlier. It was the church of his father, the goldsmith Apollos Rivoire, who later changed his name to Paul Revere; and of his mother, Deborah Hitchbourn. Born in France, the elder Revere was the first of his family to come to Boston.

But the Hitchbourns and other branches of the family—Patishalls, Dexters, and Woodys—had been in North America almost since the beginning of English colonization.

There were many of them throughout Boston and the rest of New England. Some of them spent their lives challenging authority. They fought the French, the Indians, themselves, and Captain Mackintosh's South End Gang. One or two were clapped in jail for their brawling. A few managed to stay one step ahead of the law. Most of them, however, were hard working and quite respectable.

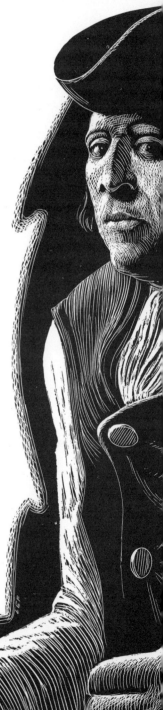

From his spirited middle-class ancestors, French and English alike, Paul Revere inherited a stubborn passion for protest. His eagerness to challenge superior power—power that dared to impose unreasonable restrictions upon his personal liberties—drew him into the inner circle of Boston radicals.

His strong leadership of the North End made this burly versatile man —silversmith, engraver, dentist, and what not—welcome in every secret society in Boston. Paul Revere belonged to them all—the Sons of Liberty, the North End Caucus, St. Andrew's Masonic Lodge, Warren's Watchers, and the very exclusive, upper-class Long Room. In secret meetings held in the back rooms of the Green Dragon and the Salutation, or above the printing shop of the *Boston Gazette,* Paul Revere sat with Boston's revolutionaries, plotting to overthrow the British government in Massachusetts.

Now he stood in the wide shadow of the Cockerel. The street lamps were dark. There was a strict rule that on bright nights of the full moon the lamps were to remain unlighted. Such a moon was now beginning to rise into the cloudless night sky. Revere looked about and listened. Nothing seemed to stir. All seemed clear. He sprinted across Word Street and was on his way to Doctor Warren. He followed a crooked course that would take him a little longer, but there was no direct path to Warren's house tonight. He was not anxious to be seen by any of the King's troops.

By the time he reached Dock Square, his eyes were tearing from the wind. He stopped to catch his breath and then turned up Union Street, heading straight for Hanover and Doctor Warren.

A few minutes later he was at Warren's door, knocking. It was about ten o'clock.

For the third time that evening, Warren hurried to the door. For the third time he opened it. There, before him, stood Revere.

"Thank God," he murmured. "Come in, my friend, come in."

"What news?" Revere asked anxiously.

"The Regulars are out!" Warren said excitedly. "And they are going out by water! I learned of the river crossing only a few minutes ago!"

Quickly, as they moved from the front hall into the parlor, Joseph Warren outlined the events of the past hour. Revere was not surprised to hear about the arrest warrants for Adams and Hancock. He agreed that it had been wise to send Billy Dawes over the Neck to Lexington to warn the two leaders to flee.

Then Warren and Revere discussed the signal to Charlestown.

"We cannot be sure that our signal lanterns will be seen," said Warren. "If you can possibly get across the river, you should. They will be expecting you in Charlestown."

"I am ready to leave at once," replied Revere.

"Billy may not be able to reach Lexington," Warren continued. "If you manage to reach Charlestown, Paul, I want you to ride to Lexington also. Warn Adams and Hancock that they must seek safer ground immediately. Then move on to Concord. Alert the people there. Sound the alarm everywhere that Gage is on the move! With both you and Billy

32

riding express, one of you is bound to get through."

"Have no fear, doctor," said Revere. "We shall aim our lights at Charlestown before Gage's troops are across the river. Let us pray that our lanterns are seen. If all goes well, I shall see to the safety of our friends in Lexington with time to spare."

The men shook hands and exchanged farewells.

Paul Revere retraced his crooked path back to Word Street. There he hesitated. He wondered whether to return home for a warm coat, boots, and spurs—things he would need for the night's ride—or to continue to the north corner of Sheafe and Salem where he expected to find Rob Newman.

He decided to go on to meet Newman. The lantern signal could not wait.

As he expected, the young sexton was there.

"The Regulars are out by water!" Revere told him. "Show two lanterns!"

Revere then doubled back to Middle Street, entered the rear yard of the Cockerel through a side path, and sped across the open space to his own back door. Rachel let him in. He kissed his wife affectionately on the cheek as he brushed by her. His mother was still swaying back and forth in the creaky rocking chair. Young Paul was there. So was Revere's

17-year-old daughter Deborah. None of them spoke. The rest of the children had been put to bed. The dog lay quietly near the back door. It was almost half past ten.

Revere grunted as he began to pull on his boots. "The Regulars are crossing the river," he said. "There'll be trouble. I've got some outdoor work to do tonight. I shall try to return as soon as I can. There's no cause to worry about me." He grunted again. At last the boots were on.

Paul Revere, still hunched over, looked at his family. He adored them all. But whatever loving thoughts he had, he kept to himself.

Finally, he rose. "I have no minutes left, dear girl," he said to Rachel. "None of us do."

Turning to his son, he said, "Mind the estate, boy."

With one parting look at his silent family, Paul Revere pulled on his overcoat and slipped out the back door to find Josh Bentley, Tom Richardson, and his hidden rowboat.

Unnoticed, his dog slipped out after him.

Rachel approached the door as her husband once again faded into the wide shadow of the Cockerel—his dog close behind. She held two shiny objects in her hands.

"He forgot his spurs," she said softly. "He'll be wanting them."

General Thomas Gage

About an hour earlier and less than a mile from Paul Revere's house, General Thomas Gage stood at a window in Province House, the elegant three-story brick residence of the royal governors. He saw nothing. The night hung from the star-strewn sky like an endless black curtain. He cocked his head to listen for sounds outside. He heard nothing but the windy rattling of the window glass. He remained there for a minute or two. Finally, he turned away, strode across the room and put his back to a crackling fire.

It was almost half past nine. The busy comings and goings at Province House during the long day had slowed down. Most of the activity was now at the south end of Boston Common, the great green field beside the Charles River. Soon the first troops would arrive and fall in with waiting companies of Grenadiers and Light Infantry. Within the next hour 700 crack soldiers of King George III's Regular Army would be ready to cross the river to teach the Yankee farmers that America belonged to England.

Only a few staff officers remained near the general. They were leaning over a large table in the center of the room, murmuring over a clutter of maps and papers. Thomas Gage blankly watched them, heedless of the scorching fire. His mind was on the flotilla of longboats rocking in the choppy water. Some of them were beached, being prepared for boarding. In another hour, the gathering force on the Common would be slowly towed downstream, their longboats lashed together in small groups.

Gage's thoughts passed on across the river to the Cambridge marshes—to Phip's farm, a place near Lechmere Point where the troops would land. From there they would march about twenty miles to Concord, destroy the colonial arms supply, arrest Sam Adams and John Hancock —if they could be found—and return to Boston. General Gage, always the careful planner, measured every step along the way in his mind.

Gage was a cautious general. He counted on absolute secrecy to surprise the radicals—to catch them off guard before they could respond. Of course the rebels expected something. But when and where was Gage's own secret—so he had thought.

Earlier in the evening, one of his regimental commanders, Lord Percy, had come to him with a disquieting report. Percy had overheard a group of colonials talking about the coming raid on Concord—a raid that was supposed to be a secret. Now they knew, according to Percy. Gage, who disliked fighting altogether, was suddenly faced with the possibility that the colonial militia would take up arms against his professional troops. If so, it was too late to avoid a battle.

What if Percy is right? he thought. What if the provincials do know our purpose? What then? Will they resist? They would not dare tempt the power of the British nation! We shall have Concord, Hancock, and Adams. Sam Adams—that misbegotten rabble-rousing brewmaster! Sam Adams—that devil above all! We must not miss our aim! We must have it all and be done with it!

For an instant, the general's brief visit to London, a year earlier, crossed his mind. The King was enraged over the Boston Tea Party.

"Blows must decide whether they are to be subjects of this country or independent," wrote King George III to his Prime Minister, Lord North.

Parliament, too, was outraged over the affair. "The town of Boston ought to be knocked about its ears," shouted one member of the House of Commons. "You'll never meet with the proper obedience to the laws of this country until you have destroyed that nest of locusts."

Determined to punish Massachusetts, the King sent for the Commander in Chief of all his forces in America, General Thomas Gage.

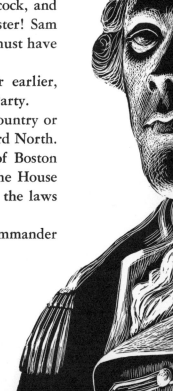

The pleasant, likable general, the son of a viscount, was very much at ease among the aristocrats of London. He attended a number of balls and dinners with his American-born wife and amused the guests with humorous military stories. His clear, blue eyes would twinkle when he solemnly informed them, "My officers call me the Old Woman, but to my private soldiers I am plain Tommy." Rarely would he discuss the colonial situation, except to point out what cowards the colonists were.

"They will be lions as long as we are lambs," he told King George. "If we take the resolute part, they will prove to be very meek."

The King liked what he heard. He appointed General Gage royal governor of Massachusetts. Gage protested. He knew nothing about politics, he complained. The King waved off Gage's protests and sent him back to Boston to subdue the unruly colonists with troops.

But once back in America, Gage was slow to act. He had hoped that the colonists would appreciate his reluctance to use force against them and would stop their rebellious activities.

"Meek indeed," Gage now grumbled to himself, a year later. "These are different times."

And now we take the resolute part, he thought. No doubt our secretaries for war and these colonies will be greatly relieved of their anxieties when they learn that our misbehaving cousins have been relieved of their gunpowder by His Majesty's Boston garrison—so many months idle, in their eyes. I've had enough of their letters and orders, whinings and urgings. What perspective can they have on my situation? None! No matter, before the sun sets tomorrow we shall have put an end . . .

The general's thoughts were interrupted by the arrival of a young ensign. James Archer stood rigid and stared straight ahead as the door swiftly closed behind him.

"Ensign James Archer, sir. Fifty-ninth Nova Scotia, sir," he barked to no one in particular. "I present the compliments of my commander, sir, and request permission to submit his report on the condition of his station, sir."

Colonel Stephen Kemble, Gage's intelligence chief, moved toward the ensign to take the report. The condition of the Fifty-ninth Regiment on the Boston Neck and its immediate approaches was important to the

success of the Concord raid. No matter how well known his plan was inside Boston, if no one outside the city knew about it Gage could still maintain an element of surprise.

The nine o'clock curfew on river crossings made it nearly impossible for anyone to ferry over to the mainland with the news. The only other way for someone to spread the alarm that the British were moving was to sneak overland—over the Neck and through the town gate. If no one had passed through, then the British could be reasonably certain that no one outside Boston would expect the marching of troops at this particular hour.

Colonel Kemble listened to the ensign's report. Finally Kemble turned to General Gage. "Sir, the situation on the Neck is secure. No one has been permitted exit since nightfall. Ensign Archer also reports three desertions from the regiment sometime during the day. I believe this now makes a total of eleven for the Fifty-ninth since last Saturday. There were twelve all told, but one of these was picked up near Roxbury. He'll soon have his back creased by the lash."

General Gage frowned. The less he heard about desertions and the lash, the better he liked it. There were altogether too many of his soldiers fleeing camp. Some of them were even drilling the colonial militia. His men were restless and ill-tempered. It was becoming increasingly difficult to maintain discipline among the troops in Boston, trapped and bored as they were in a city where they were clearly unwelcome. They had been there for almost a year and many would do anything to leave— even at the risk of being caught and subjected to swift, brutal military punishment.

"A good, cold night march should be splendid medicine," Gage said. "It will stir the blood and stretch the legs. Perhaps our adventure to and from Concord will have some extra benefits."

Gage personally thanked the young officer for his report and asked him to convey his compliments to the entire regiment. Kemble dismissed the ensign and turned to say something to Gage, but the general was poking the fire with a brass-handled rod. Kemble hesitated, shrugged, and returned to the group around the table.

"The Old Woman is distant tonight," Major Caine, an aide, remarked

to Kemble. The two officers turned and took another look at Thomas Gage.

As the fire snapped and sparked, its fluttering light danced across the general's uniform. His white knee breeches were a dozen shades of orange. His polished boots reflected the leaping flames so brilliantly that it appeared as if the fire was climbing right up his legs. His jacket was a gaudy pattern of red cloth, black trim, and flashing gold braid. He almost seemed to be ablaze.

It was about 10:15. The fire began to die. Captain Gabriel Maturin, Gage's personal secretary, came over and hurled a huge split log into the fireplace. The sparks flew at the general's head with the sound of cracking rifles.

"My apologies, sir," said Maturin as he backed away from the noise.

General Gage did not budge. His gaze was far away. Maturin thought he looked old and tired beyond his fifty-seven years. General Sir Frederick Haldimand, Gage's Swiss-born deputy commander, joined his chief at the fireplace.

Gage stabbed at the fire, loosening charred bits of wood and watching them fall into the glowing pile of ashes. The memory of twenty years of American service in a career spanning thirty-four years in the British army flickered through his mind.

"Taxes and tyranny, riots and murder, arson and treason," Gage grumbled to Haldimand. "They petitioned this and they petitioned that —ten years of it! I warned the Crown that they were taking great strides toward independency."

"Still, you have been patient in the face of much slander and disobedience," replied Sir Frederick.

"By what right do they press us so?" continued Gage. "These provinces are British colonies, not independent states! Have I not tried to bring them to their senses in the most conciliatory manner? And the town children! What about them? Did I not take fatherly pains to heed their grievances against the King's soldiers?"

"Indeed you have," answered Haldimand. "Now they play in peace, unmolested, without fear of a prickly bayonet in their backsides."

"Yes, and now where are we?" asked Gage. "I'll tell you where!

40

Fenced inside this nasty little peninsula, the gate locked shut—4,000 of the King's best with 15,000 surly provincials and a flock of sniveling loyalists. And thousands more provincials, from Carolina to Massachusetts, ready to cuff us into the sea if they can. Oh, they'll fight. Not tomorrow—they would not dare. But the fight is coming. What will they gain? Nothing! We shall subdue them in the end."

Haldimand agreed. Gage said no more. He sat down in a high-back chair that hid his bulky frame from nearly everyone in the room. Sir Frederick excused himself. As he crossed the room to rejoin the other officers at the cluttered table, a messenger appeared. He addressed himself to Haldimand.

"The first companies are away, sir."

"The first companies?" asked Haldimand with surprise.

"Yes, sir, the first companies. Twelve, sir," he replied. "We cannot make it in one crossing."

"Why not?" demanded Sir Frederick.

"The navy did not provide enough boats, sir," came the answer.

General Gage, overhearing the report, leaped to his feet.

"Let Admiral Graves be careless with his own expeditions, not mine," he growled angrily. "If we are not in Concord by sunrise, Graves will answer for it. Take that message back with you," Gage ordered the startled messenger.

The soldier hurried out of the room. Thomas Gage turned to his fire once more and sat down.

The flames continued to seer the crisply burning wood. The logs settled lower in the grate. The pile of ashes grew and smouldered.

Gage suddenly became uneasy about the outcome of tonight's march on Concord. His thoughts flashed back to the day he made the decision to use military force. It was three days earlier—Saturday, April 15.

Before daybreak on Saturday, he was awakened by Colonel Kemble, Major Caine, and Captain Maturin. They spoke in hushed voices.

"Are you awake, sir?"

"Yes, yes. What is it?" Gage propped himself up on his elbows.

"We have an urgent message from Church."

"Where is he? Have him come in."

"He would not show himself, sir. We do not know his whereabouts."

Gage, his shaven skull hidden under a dazzling red silk nightcap, jerked himself upward and blinked at his visitors. A message from Doctor Benjamin Church was worth listening to, even at this ungodly hour.

Unknown to his fellow members of the Sons of Liberty and the Provincial Congress, Doctor Benjamin Church was a spy for the British. From the day when General Gage landed in Boston to punish the people, Church began to spy regularly for the British, reporting directly to General Gage.

A number of patriots had vague suspicions about the high-living doctor. He was seen coming out of Gage's office several times. On more than one occasion he dined openly with British officers in public taverns. When questioned, he always had a perfect reason.

Now Colonel Kemble quickly told General Gage about the urgent message from Church.

"Doctor Church informs us that the Provincial Congress will vote, probably today, to raise a large army. Enlistments will be sought in all the colonies. French assistance may be sought. The New Englanders are better armed than we supposed. The town militias will be ready to attack any British column moving out of Boston with baggage wagons and cannon. There are thousands of Minutemen standing by."

"We must put an end to these ambitions, and promptly," Gage said. "Have warrants issued for the arrest of Hancock, Sam Adams, and Warren. No, not Warren—not yet. We shall stir up a hornet's nest if we take him now. I shall settle for Adams and Hancock. Find them!"

"Yes, sir," replied Kemble.

"Call a full staff and regimental meeting for eight o'clock this morning," continued Gage. "I want the navy here, too."

At exactly eight o'clock General Gage in full uniform—a powdered wig replacing his nightcap—flanked by his personal staff, greeted his commanders. He had a firm, quick handshake for each of the officers as they filed into the room. Altogether about thirty high-ranking officers crowded the room. They represented the entire military and naval es-

44

tablishment of Boston—twelve infantry regiments, the naval squadron, the royal engineers, the marines, the artillery, and the general staff.

"Gentlemen," Gage began, "I learned this morning that the provincials are to recruit an army of some strength and will take up arms to gain their ends. I propose to stop them before they do."

"The Old Woman has finally made up his mind," someone whispered.

Gage, unaware of the remark, continued. "It is time to put to rest any attempt against His Majesty's will, purpose, law, and property in this colony. We shall prepare, with all haste and secrecy, to spoil or take the large provincial collection of weapons, powder, and other war devices at Concord. We shall destroy their means to obstruct His Majesty's presence in these colonies.

"I have ordered the arrest of Samuel Adams and John Hancock. I have decided to move a strong force across the river at night. It is the shortest and fastest route to Concord. Admiral Graves, you will provide the necessary boats and oarsmen for the crossing. I want to be able to move tonight if I have to—certainly within the next day or two.

"I have not, as yet, chosen the field command. I expect to do so shortly.

45

Colonel Kemble will have further instructions for you at the conclusion of this meeting. That will be all, gentlemen. Thank you."

As the officers left the room, General Gage turned to Sir Frederick Haldimand. "Well, Sir Frederick," he said, "this should put the lie to the 'Old Woman,' now, don't you think? I have always preferred to be called 'Tommy' behind my back. It has a small grain of affection in it. Not much, mind you, but enough."

Gage, still seated in his high-back chair before the fire, smiled to himself as he recalled the look of surprise on Haldimand's face. But his smile quickly faded as the memory of Saturday, April 15, dissolved in the smoke and spark of the fire. Today, Tuesday, April 18, was much fresher in his mind.

The general remembered, vividly, awakening with anticipation. He had scowled with disappointment as he watched a chilling rain streak his bedroom window. The morning weather was intolerable. It was worse than yesterday's soggy drizzle and prevented him from ordering the raid to begin. Gage could not wait much longer.

He did not act on Saturday night, the fifteenth, as he thought he might, because more preparations were needed. He did not order the raid for Sunday night, because he feared the damp weather that had already begun to settle over the area. Moreover, it was undesirable to disturb the Sunday sabbath with a major military assault. Monday's drizzle was unfortunate. Now, today, Tuesday morning, there was more of the same—rain.

By noon, however, the air seemed lighter. The rain slackened. Gage walked rapidly to a window as the sky broke clear. In minutes the low scudding clouds disappeared, chased by a brisk east wind. Soon the sky gleamed bright and blue. Tonight would be clear. The ground would be dry and hard. Tonight would be the time to strike.

General Thomas Gage began to write the order.

"Having received Intelligence, that a Quantity of Ammunition, Provision, Artillery, Tents and small Arms, have been collected at Concord, for the Avowed Purpose of raising and supporting a Rebellion against His Majesty, you will . . . march . . . seize . . . destroy. . . ."

The general addressed the order to "Lieutenant Colonel Francis Smith, Tenth Regiment Foot." The stout Colonel Smith was not the most efficient officer in the Boston garrison. Nevertheless, it was customary for the ranking senior field officer to be chosen for command of such an expedition. Smith was that man. Gage was acting according to British military tradition.

Gage next gave orders to deploy an advanced detachment—about twenty men—along the main roads between Cambridge and Concord. He wanted these roads blocked. All horsemen, couriers, and persons unknown were to be turned back or detained for questioning.

The men of the detachment should try to learn the exact whereabouts of Adams and Hancock. Colonel Kemble thought that the two patriot leaders were in or near Lexington. He passed that information on to the officer in charge of the detachment, Major Edward Mitchell.

"Have this party out well before sunset today," Gage ordered. "See to

it that they are carrying the arrest warrants. The patrol should be well armed but cloaked. The less uniform seen before we march, the better.''

Late in the afternoon Gage summoned Colonel Smith and formally placed him in command of the 700-man raiding force. Major John Pitcairn, a tough, seasoned marine, would be second in command.

General Gage handed Smith a packet of orders and maps. The general carefully explained that there were to be no cannon or baggage wagons in the line of march or anywhere near it.

"We have reliable information that if these things are present, the rebels will fire upon the column. I should like to avoid any blood-letting. I have no desire to war against these people. Nor do I wish them to war against me. We are Englishmen, one and all.''

Gage told his field commander that the 1,000-man First Brigade under Lord Percy would be ready to come to Smith's assistance should he require it. This was standard military precaution. With a handshake, he wished Smith well and saw him to the door.

Gage then saw Lord Percy and, soon after, joined his wife for dinner in the stately dining room of Province House. The general returned directly to his office after dinner.

Now, an hour and a half later, Thomas Gage seemed to sag in his chair before the roasting fire. His hand shook slightly as he pulled a silver watch from his waistcoat pocket. The timepiece was silent. It had stopped some time ago. The general rose slowly from his chair, annoyed at the failure of the watch. He glanced at a large grandfather clock ticking away on the other side of the room and then reset his watch. It was just past 10:40.

Gage turned to his officers at the table. "How do we stand?" he asked.

"Sir, the boats of the first shuttle have not returned," replied Lieutenant Rooke, a young aide who had entered the room as Gage was resetting his watch. "We expect they will not be back for another half-hour. With any luck at all, sir, we should have the entire force across not long after midnight.''

The general grunted. "I trust we shall be well along the road before the whole countryside knows of our coming. Any word on Adams and Hancock?''

"No word yet, sir.''

48

"Gentlemen, there is no need for me to keep the vigil. I am retiring. Be certain to inform me of any unusual occurrences.

"I hope that we shall have these troublesome events peacefully settled in due course. I have a great fondness for our American cousins, as I do for Englishmen everywhere. I know that many Americans hold me in the same regard. These are unhappy times."

Gage was tired. The strain of the last few days was evident.

"Nevertheless," he continued, "I have a solemn obligation to uphold the laws of Great Britain, follow the advice of His Majesty's Minister for these colonies, and carry out the orders of the Secretary for War. All this I do now, however tardy it may seem to some. Good night, gentlemen. God save the King!"

"Good night, sir."

"God save the King, sir!"

Sexton Robert Newman

About 9:45 that same evening, Paul Revere's messenger was inching his way along the side of Mrs. Newman's house at the corner of Sheafe and Salem Streets.

As he ducked under a beam of light coming from a partially shuttered window, a wave of laughter seemed to escape from inside the house. The fitful sound soared over the rooftops, sucked upward by the wind. It hovered over the head of the stranger and then floated away.

Curious, he ducked back under the window. He readjusted his muffler to hide his face and slowly, ever so slowly, raised his head to see what he could.

Inside were a number of British officers lounging about. Several of them were playing cards. Their uniforms were unbuttoned, their pistols and swords nowhere in sight. Some were without their wigs. One was in his shirtsleeves. Another was without his boots. None of them seemed to be going anywhere—least of all to Concord—that night.

On a table against a far wall stood a half-dozen bottles of wine. The Britons were surrounded by goblets—or so it seemed to the silent observer outside. Some were almost full. Some were empty. One officer was draining his glass. A large cheese ball, already savored, waited on another table closer to the center of the room.

Straddling a chair nearby, looking off into space, was Mrs. Newman's 23-year-old son Robert. He was waiting—as he had been waiting

51

since Sunday night—for a signal from Mr. Revere to light the lanterns in the belfry of Christ Church.

As the messenger watched, Mrs. Newman, smiling, entered the room. She was apparently enjoying the party. She caught her son's attention and shook her head as if to say, "Not yet."

The messenger saw the signal and was reminded that he had a job to do. Once again he ducked under the lighted window and quickly walked around to the back of the house. There he found the open window that Paul Revere had mentioned. It framed a small room faintly lit by a single candle.

He did not have long to wait. Mrs. Newman slipped into the room within a minute or two.

The messenger whistled softly.

Mrs. Newman heard the noise but made no move.

He whistled again.

Now she walked quickly to the window.

"Mr. Revere will be along soon," he whispered. "He has been delayed a bit. Have Rob wait at the corner of Sheafe and Salem."

Mrs. Newman turned and silently left the room. The messenger had done his work. Now he was through for the night.

Mrs. Newman smilingly re-entered her parlor. She carried a tray of small cakes for her uninvited guests—the British officers who lived in her house under the terms of the Quartering Act. Despite her smiles and graciousness, Mrs. Newman hated the British for this invasion of her home and her privacy.

Again she caught the attention of her son Robert. This time she nodded. Robert stretched, yawned, and got off his chair.

"I'm very tired," he announced. "If you gentlemen will excuse me, I am off to bed."

"Tired?" questioned one officer.

"To bed?" asked another.

"He needs his rest," answered his mother, "what with all the work the church fathers have him doing. I have one son at the organ and Rob here minding the properties. Christ Church needs them both—rested and fit."

"But he's young, madam. The moon is young. Why, he hasn't even sipped a gram of this marvelous port with us. Have some, my boy, have some. This will give you more strength than your pillow."

The Englishman filled a goblet for Newman, who refused it.

"Drink it!" demanded the officer, who now held Rob by the arm. "To the King!"

"To the King," answered Robert Newman, and he sipped the wine.

The officer loosened his iron grip. "That's better, my boy," he said, and staggered back to his friends.

Newman took another sip to avoid trouble, put down the glass, slowly bowed to the company as he backed away.

"Goodnight, gentlemen," he added.

"Sweet dreams," one of them called. "Remember the King in your bedtime prayers." They all laughed. "You'd better save a few 'God Blesses' for your countrymen. They'll need them after tonight." They all roared at this.

Mrs. Newman, meanwhile, tried to attract Rob's attention again. She wanted to tell him that Revere would be delayed—that Robert should wait at the corner. But Rob left the room too quickly. He was upstairs in his bedroom before she could give him the message.

Softly, he slipped the bolt into place and stood in the dark, listening to the laughter drifting up from the floor below. He quietly cursed the Englishmen who were on their way to drinking themselves senseless. Then noiselessly he moved across the room, put on his coat, and crawled through a window to an adjoining rooftop. He crept along for several yards, found the footing he wanted, and dropped to the grassy ground.

There he expected to find Paul Revere waiting, as they had planned it on Sunday. But Mr. Revere was not there. Confused, Rob worked his way around to Sheafe Street.

It was about 10:20. Rob Newman was beginning to regret being mixed up in this tricky business when Paul Revere suddenly appeared at the corner. Rob approached the square, solid, coatless figure of Revere.

"The Regulars are out by water!" said Revere. "Show two lanterns!" Then the older man hurried away.

Newman looked about. The way was clear. He crossed Salem Street to Christ Church. As he fumbled in his pockets for the key to unlock the door, two cloaked figures came up behind him, startling him. They were John Pulling and Tom Barnard. Rob Newman had forgotten that these two Sons of Liberty were to stand guard for him.

The young sexton's hands were trembling now. He had more difficulty than before in locating the large brass key. At last he found it, yanked

it out of his pocket, and dropped it. The metallic clatter seemed to ring from one end of Salem Street to the other.

"We're for it now!" Barnard groaned. The three of them got on their knees and searched for it.

"I've got it!" called Newman.

"For God's sake, be still," commanded Pulling. "Open the door before you wake the dead, with us among them."

Newman unlocked the door. They moved inside, closing the heavy door after them.

"Wait. Make no move," Pulling whispered. "I want to be certain that no one is here."

John Pulling and Robert Newman were members of the congregation of this handsome Anglican church, and Pulling was a vestryman. Half of the congregation was loyal to the King, while the other half favored the patriots. The three men were anxious to get on with their night's work—but they were not anxious to be observed by any Tories.

John Pulling walked rapidly under the gallery and down the left aisle toward the altar, looking into each high box pew as he went by. As he passed the pew of General Thomas Gage, he shook his fist but kept right on moving. He turned, glanced at the pulpit above him, craned his neck as he looked over the altar rail, and turned again to look down the center aisle.

Moonlight had begun to filter through the windows. It highlighted the doves of peace fixed to the brass chandeliers suspended from the ceiling. The organ pipes at the far end were quiet. Pulling gazed at the trumpeting angels that flanked the royal coat of arms above the organ pipes. At the sight of the coat of arms, he shook his fist once more. Then he checked all the pews in the second aisle until he reached Newman and Barnard still standing at the door.

"We are alone," Pulling said. "All is well. We'll have the lamps now, Rob."

Newman groped in a dark closet and pulled out two lanterns. He had placed them in readiness after the Sunday night meeting at the Green Dragon Tavern.

"I'm going back outside," Pulling declared, "to keep watch on the

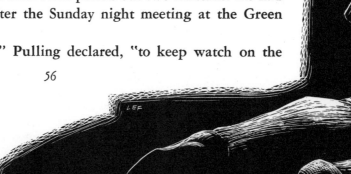

street. I'll warn you of any danger. Tom, you stay where you are—inside—just behind the door."

John Pulling stepped outside, and Barnard shut the door.

Robert Newman began to climb the steep, narrow wooden stairway that led up the belfry to the very top.

It was now about half past ten. General Gage was sitting in his high-back chair before the fireplace in Province House. Half of his troops were somewhere on the windy, moon-flecked waters of the Charles River. They would not wade ashore for at least another half-hour. The rest of Gage's assault force stood on the cold, wind-swept Common, waiting their turn to cross the river.

Paul Revere, at this moment, was leaving his house for the second time that evening. He was on his way to meet Josh Bentley and Tom Richardson, who would attempt to row him to Charlestown.

Billy Dawes was across the Neck. A soldier of the Fifty-ninth Regiment had relaxed his guard long enough—and against all orders—to allow Billy (pretending to be a homeward-bound drunken farmer) to

pass beyond the town gate. Now Dawes was riding like a demon for Lexington on his borrowed horse.

Robert Newman was climbing up the tower of Christ Church, higher and higher, hardly able to see a thing in the dark stairway. The lanterns banged against each other and echoed up and down the stairway. He lost his balance trying to keep them quiet. He stumbled. But still he climbed. He reached the great bell loft and stopped to catch his breath.

The brick-and-wood bell tower of Christ Church, with its high steeple capped by Shem Drowne's weathervane, stood taller than any other structure in town. It rose high above Copp's Hill because several wealthy English merchants in Central America, desiring a good Boston landmark for their ships, paid for the soaring spire.

A few more feet straight up. Now Robert Newman looked out of the loftiest window in Boston.

Ahead of him, to the north, lay Charlestown. There, too, were Colonel Conant and the other patriots waiting for Robert Newman's signal to tell them that the British were on the march and what route they were taking out of Boston. The young sexton could see the *Somerset,* blocking the mouth of the river. To the west, the British longboats were nearing the Cambridge shore.

Far below Robert Newman, Josh Bentley and Tom Richardson were crouching in the shadow of a tombstone in the graveyard, waiting to row Mr. Revere across the river to Charlestown. Paul Revere was now running along Princes Street, followed by his dog, too intent on reaching his two comrades and his hidden rowboat to look up at the steeple of the church.

All around Rob Newman was the wind, whistling and buffeting the steeple. Moonlight flooded the small space.

Carefully he hung the two lanterns. He fished a small tinderbox, with flint and steel, from his pocket and raised a flame with his first strike. With trembling hands, he quickly lit a candle in each of the two lanterns.

The lanterns burned brightly through the clear night.

There—the signal was given!

The British were moving out by water.

A minute or so later, Robert Newman extinguished both lanterns—afraid to let them burn any longer, fearful of arousing British suspicions. He left the darkened lanterns in the belfry and started back down the tower.

At Province House, behind General Thomas Gage, the flames in the fireplace sputtered. The wind outside had changed its direction. Now it blew inland from the southeast. Above him, another weather vane fashioned by Shem Drowne—a glittering golden Indian on the cupola of Province House—slowly turned to the northwest. It fixed its glassy, moonlit eye on the distant targets. Its great bow and arrow wavered in the wind, aiming first at Lexington, then at Concord.

Tomorrow, Wednesday—April 19, 1775—would be a cool, clear day, touched by the gentle sweetness of spring.

Tomorrow would be war.

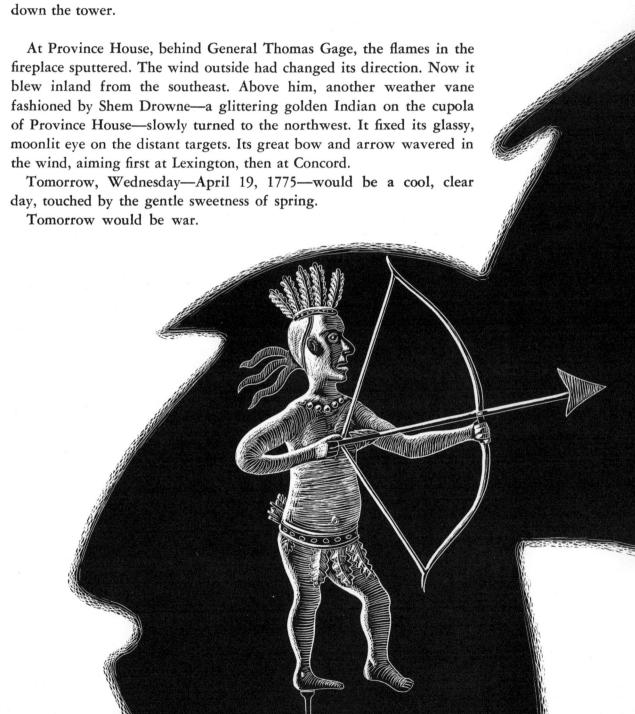

Epilogue

The Charlestown patriots saw Robert Newman's brief signal. Billy Dawes and Paul Revere, after arousing much of the countryside, both got through to Sam Adams and John Hancock in Lexington. Adams and Hancock escaped in time. The British never found them.

Revere and Dawes, joined by Doctor Samuel Prescott, rode on to Concord to warn the patriots there. They were stopped by a British patrol. Prescott and Dawes escaped. In the excitement, Billy fell off his horse but found his way back to Boston. Prescott reached Concord.

Revere was released by the British patrol but they kept his horse. He walked back to the Clarke house in Lexington just in time to accompany Adams and Hancock to a place not far out of town. He returned to Buckman's Tavern in Lexington where Hancock kept a trunk full of valuable papers. There he helped John Lowell, Hancock's personal secretary, remove the trunk to the Clarke house for safekeeping.

As the two men were dragging the trunk across the Lexington Green, half of the British force—between 300 and 400 men—arrived under the command of Major Pitcairn. They were challenged by 77 Minutemen lined up on the Green. Someone fired a shot. The British charged. Eight Minutemen were killed. Ten were wounded. The British, unscathed, marched on to Concord. There they were soon joined by Colonel Smith and the remainder of the expeditionary force.

Revere and Lowell, meanwhile, had hidden Hancock's trunk in the Clarke house. Revere remained somewhere nearby until the following day, when he made his way back to Cambridge.

At Concord the British found little to destroy. The colonists had safely relocated most of their supplies. The British officers sat around drinking brandy while the troops remained in formation in the center of town. By this time—about nine o'clock in the morning—Smith began to realize that the entire countryside was up in arms. This was more than he had bargained for. He sent for reinforcements.

As he awaited the arrival of Lord Percy and the First Brigade's relief column, Smith tried to destroy the North Concord Bridge. A skirmish followed. The British lost.

Smith decided that the situation was growing dangerous. There was a possibility that the gathering colonials would trap the British in Concord. Smith ordered a speedy return to Charlestown by way of Lexington. He began the withdrawal at noon. All along the short route to Lexington, the redcoats, now greatly outnumbered, fell victim to deadly American crossfire.

Staggered by the ferocity of the American attack, Smith's exhausted, panic-stricken assault force stumbled into Lord Percy and the First Brigade outside of Lexington. The badly mauled British finally reached Charlestown later that same night, pursued by about 15,000 colonials. During the ordeal, 278 Englishmen were killed, wounded, or missing. Among the wounded was Lieutenant Colonel Francis Smith.

Ninety-six Americans fell that afternoon of April 19.

Sometime after midnight of the nineteenth, a few hours after sending Revere to Charlestown, Doctor Joseph Warren attended the birth of a baby. But he did not remain long at the mother's bedside. He took the morning's first ferry to the mainland and headed for Cambridge. The next day he unexpectedly ran into Paul Revere and Doctor Benjamin Church, who were returning from the battlegrounds.

Warren set up new headquarters for the Massachusetts Committee of Safety. He began to organize the thousands of armed colonials into the semblance of an army. The patriots pinned the British inside Boston and laid siege to the city.

Two months later George Washington was named Commander in Chief of the new Continental Army. Warren was appointed to the rank of major general.

On June 17 the British tried to break the siege of Boston. The battle of Bunker Hill followed. Joseph Warren took part in the battle and was killed. He was thirty-four years old.

Dead, too, at the battle of Bunker Hill, was Major John Pitcairn, the crusty British marine. He was buried in the crypt of Christ Church—better known in later years as "Old North."

General Thomas Gage publicly dismissed the Lexington-Concord expedition as a minor incident. Privately, he knew it was a disaster. Weeks later, as he watched the battle of Bunker Hill from the belfry of Christ Church, he witnessed another disaster for his troops. Soon after, Gage was relieved of his command, and he returned to England with his American wife.

Paul Revere, after pleading for a year to be appointed an officer in the Continental Army, finally received a commission in the Massachusetts militia. He was given command of an artillery unit stationed on lonely Fort Castle William Island in Boston harbor—a singularly unimportant post. Except for one disastrous American assault on the British at Penobscot, Maine, Revere remained on the island for three years. He rose to the rank of lieutenant colonel. In 1779 he was court-martialed for his part in the American defeat in Maine. He was accused of cowardice and insubordination. He was declared innocent. Nevertheless, his reputation suffered.

Revere went on to become a successful and wealthy Boston business-man after he left the service. He lived to be eighty-three years old. And all during his long later life he continued to take an active part in the public affairs of Boston. His earlier troubles with the army were forgotten and he became a much idolized figure—one of the last surviving heroes of the American Revolution.

Doctor Benjamin Church, the informer for the British, became director-general of hospitals for George Washington's Continental Army. But in September 1775 he was arrested, tried, and convicted of treason. General Washington himself presided at the trial. Church was not executed but imprisoned. Eventually he was put aboard a ship bound for the West Indies. The ship was lost in a storm.

A few seconds after Robert Newman extinguished his signal lanterns in the belfry, a British patrol approached Christ Church where John Pulling was standing guard. Pulling fled and safely hid himself in an empty wine barrel. Whether or not Barnard stayed behind the church door long enough to warn Newman is not known. However, Newman managed to leave the church unseen, returning home safely.

The British found out about the lantern signal to Charlestown. They arrested several men including Robert Newman. He was questioned and released. The British did not pursue the matter further.

Sam Adams served Massachusetts in the Continental Congress until the end of the Revolutionary War. He was later elected governor of Massachusetts. However, his influence greatly declined from the end of the war in 1781 until his death in 1803. The new generation of politicians considered him an irresponsible radical. They feared his revolutionary abilities and wanted little to do with him.

John Hancock was the first patriot to sign the Declaration of Independence. He held a number of public offices, including president of the Continental Congress—a job he was well prepared for, having presided over the Massachusetts Provincial Congress. However, he wanted to be Commander in Chief of the Continental Army and was bitterly disappointed when George Washington received the commission.

As for the stranger who summoned Paul Revere to Doctor Warren's house on the night of April 18, and who went on to deliver Revere's own message to Robert Newman so faithfully—he remains a mystery to this very day.

The career of Leonard Everett Fisher, one of America's most distinguished artists, is marked by a broad range of skills. Painter, illustrator, author, educator, he was a Winchester Fellow of the Yale Art School; recipient of a Pulitzer painting prize; dean of an art school; and an army mapmaker. He is past president of one art society and a director of another.

He has illustrated his own 19 books (many of them about colonial American craftsmen) and some 175 books for other authors. The 1968 International Book Fair of Bologna, Italy, awarded him its Graphics Prize for juvenile books. His works are represented in numerous permanent collections. In 1969 the University of Oregon prepared a 30-page catalog of its Fisher collection.

He and his wife Margery live in Westport, Connecticut, with their three children.

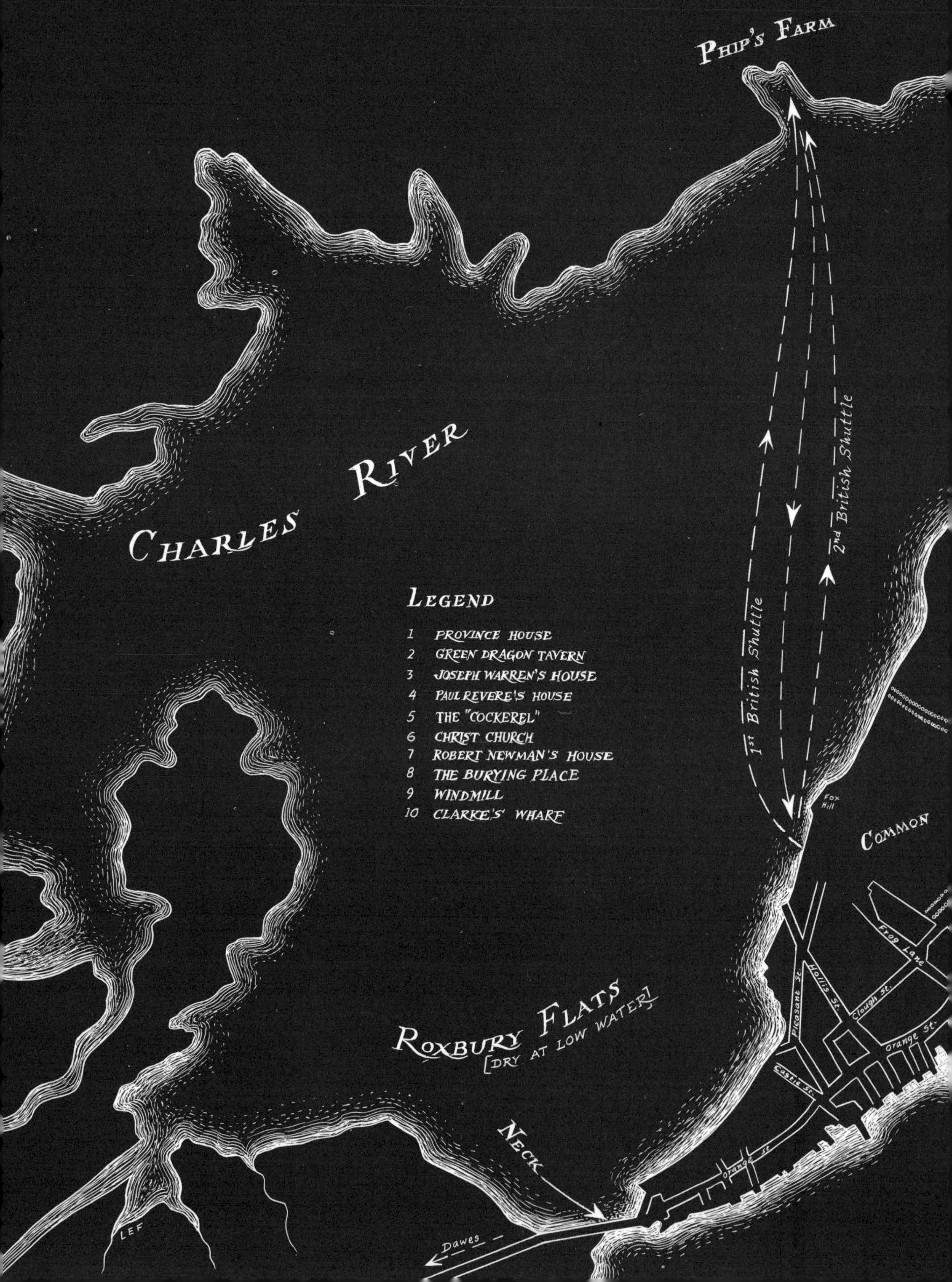

PHIP'S FARM

CHARLES RIVER

2nd British Shuttle

1st British Shuttle

LEGEND

1 PROVINCE HOUSE
2 GREEN DRAGON TAVERN
3 JOSEPH WARREN'S HOUSE
4 PAUL REVERE'S HOUSE
5 THE "COCKEREL"
6 CHRIST CHURCH
7 ROBERT NEWMAN'S HOUSE
8 THE BURYING PLACE
9 WINDMILL
10 CLARKE'S' WHARF

Fox
Hill

COMMON

Frog Lane

Pleasant St.
Hollis St.
Clough St.
Orange St.
Castle St.

ROXBURY FLATS
[DRY AT LOW WATER]

NECK

LEF

Dawes

LECHMERE PT.

BUNKER'S HILL

Breed's Hill

CHARLES RIVER

CHARLESTOWN

N

Revere

HMS Somerset

Spring St.
Gravel St.
Wiltshire St.
25
Leverett's St.
Green Lane
Southack St.
Lynn St.
Sheafe St.

Cambridge St.
Chardon St.

MILL POND

Petty way
9 8
Salem St.
Charter St.
COPP'S HILL
Lynn St.
6
Salem St.
7
North St.
Reach-more St.
Battery Alley

Grove St.
Temple St.

Hawkins St.
Hilliers Lane
Sudbury St.

Cold Lane
2
3
Back St.
Middle St.
Middle St.
5
4
Wood Lane
North sa-lem St.
Fish St.
Ship St.

Beacon Hill

Hanover St.
Court St.
Queen St.
Treamount St.
School St.
Bridge's
Dock Sq.
Union St.
Ann St.
North St.
10

Beacon St.

Won St.
Long Acre
Hanover St.
Newbury St.
Cornhill
King St.
Water St.
Mackrel Lane
Long Wharf

1
Marlborough St.
School St.
Sunset Row

Pond St.
Summer St.
Milk St.
Bishops Alley
d'Acosta's Pasture

Short St.
Essex St.

Lane Lane
Olivers St.
Battery March

Fort Hill

Cow Lane
Belchers Lane
South St.
Battery March

THE HARBOR

BOSTON
APRIL 18
1775
IN NEW ENGLAND

0   1/4   1/2   3/4   1 MILE